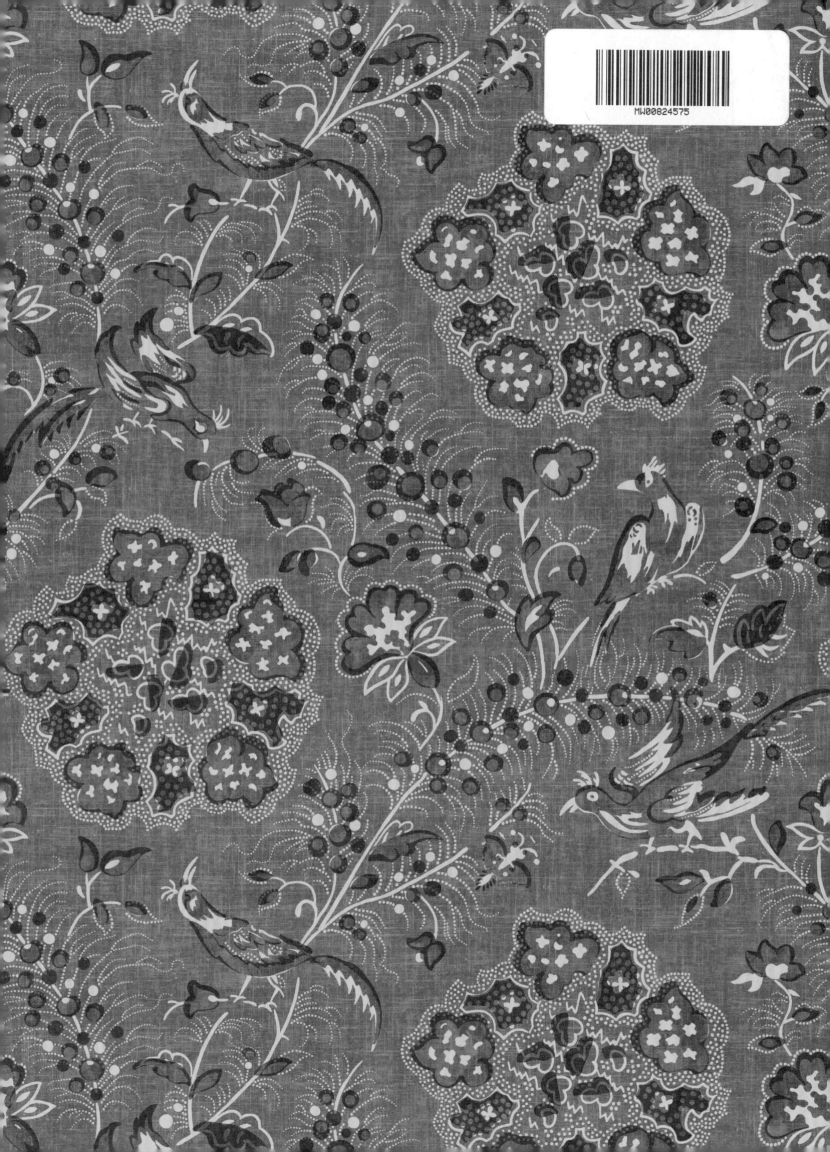

# EXTRAORDINARY INTERIORS

# SUZANNE TUCKER

## EXTRAORDINARY INTERIORS

ℳ

To my treasured clients: You entrust me with
your dreams and inner sanctums. Thank you for
allowing my vision to become a reality. For me,
you are truly the extraordinary ones.

And to my incredibly hardworking staff who
help me make those dreams come true:
These pages are a testament to your
extraordinary dedication, teamwork, and talents.

# TABLE OF CONTENTS

# INTRODUCTION

Design has so many lessons to teach us, among them that the house we think will suit us forever rarely does. My clients have always run the gamut from singles to newlyweds, from growing families to empty nesters. As a result, I have been able to explore the way design and decoration can beautifully mediate the various desires and achievements of different phases of life. So often over the years, clients who have told me "We will never move" and "This house is so me" invariably surprise themselves when their "forever" home no longer fits.

Every residence is a world unto itself, with its own personality and mood, an alchemy of culture, context, nature, nurture—all mediated through design. Geography, climate, terrain, the quality of light, and the surrounding structures obviously play key roles. So do the style of the exterior and interior architecture, the palette of materials, finishes, and colors, as well as the furnishings, fabrics, art, accessories, and the innumerable details—all the elements that make up a home. At the heart of these individual choices, however, are our experiences and memories, and the feelings and images they engender. This emotional and visual landscape is what we carry forward into our dreams of the way we want to live in our houses, whether they are small or large, single or many. This, really, is the springboard of collaboration, the place where, together with the clients and my colleagues—architects, builders, lighting experts, garden and landscape designers—my team and I enter the picture.

As a designer, I wear many hats, from armchair psychologist and mediator to archaeologist and anthropologist. I need to go deep, so I ask endless questions about matters practical and personal, tangible and intangible. My staff teasingly call me "the client whisperer" because I have developed my listening skills like a sonar. As I unearth layer after layer of meaning and

memory, of personal preferences—rituals, habits, family traditions—I gather the information that helps me transform fact, feeling, and, yes, fantasy into evocative spaces that resonate deeply and, I hope, elevate the experiences of the unique individuals who live in them.

I love how a house can seduce and captivate, how rooms can transform our knowledge of ourselves and the way we see the possible. I learned this early from growing up in the architectural and garden paradise of Santa Barbara. One of my favorite houses, belonging to family friends, was in the neoclassical style. To this day, I can visualize the vast collection of pictures hung salon-style from the floor to the twenty-foot-high ceiling. It was jaw-droppingly chic to me as a young girl.

Another vivid recollection has to do with design as theater. As a teenager, I was invited to a dinner party in a lovely old Spanish-style house in the foothills of Santa Barbara. The hosts led us through the library into a lofty, octagonal conservatory filled with ficus that touched the peak of the glass roof. Candlelight gleamed off the beautifully set table and cast shadows of the branches overhead. And peering down on us between those trees, from its place over the doorway, was a stuffed giraffe's head! In retrospect, as an animal lover, I am horrified. But to this day, my teenage memory of that room, so dramatic and exotic, still bewitches.

Over the decades, I have been fortunate to have clients just as passionate about their residences as I am. The collaborative effort between client and designer, together with architects and supporting cast members, shapes the story behind the creation of each residence. Every project within these pages tells its own variation on this universal design theme: that our homes change as our lives evolve.

In the living room of my Montecito retreat, layers of old and new overlap with disciplined order to create a kind of complex simplicity. The textiles and cotton-slipcovered furniture bring the Louis XVI mirror, once Michael Taylor's, and eighteenth-century wallpaper panel down to earth and into the now.

# FUTURE PERFECT

So often when couples become empty nesters, they decide to downsize their house. These clients, in contrast, embraced the process of upscaling to a large historic home that required a top-to-bottom renovation to serve their present and long-term needs: hosting guests, entertaining family and friends, welcoming eventual weddings and grandchildren, and creating space for their ever-growing art collection. With a stellar team, we rebuilt the property to its last square inch, establishing enfilades of rooms to capitalize on the breathtaking vistas and creating a central spiral stair surmounted by an oculus to bring natural light through the core.

This family's significant holdings of art and antiques were inspirational, as well as pivotal to every aspect of our decision-making. Certain existing pieces in their collection were a given. The rest we gradually acquired or custom-designed for the interior's scale, flow, and function. Ultimately, we assembled an outstanding array of antiques and one-of-a-kind commissioned pieces from contemporary artisans, along with further art acquisitions.

These clients love good design, whether classic or contemporary, so we used timeless elements—floor patterns and vestibules—to create intentional transitions from the public rooms to the private family rooms. Louis XVI–style paneling and moldings, bespoke and antique mantels, subtle finishes and decorative glazes, historic woodwork, and antiques mixed with art flavor the spaces with haute style. The dining room delves furthest into authenticity, with eighteenth-century Régence boiserie found in Paris that we triple-bleached for a California-casual palette. For the game room, we engaged Féau et Cie to fabricate straw marquetry walls in the art deco style of Jean-Michel Frank, an idea these clients embraced. In the family's more private spaces, we shifted color palettes and textures to create individuality and intimacy.

Outdoors, we built a romantic treillage pavilion to supplant a dilapidated carriage house. Voilà, a new destination!

OPPOSITE: Fabricated in Paris by Ateliers Saint-Jacques, the custom-designed bronze, iron, and glass front door and stair rail introduce elements of the house's pattern language and materials palette. A rare antique Scottish twelve-sided table anchors an entry hall with the client's millennia-spanning collections, which include a Ruth Asawa sculpture, a circa-1880 Japanese watercolor, and Han dynasty urns and vessels. The *faux bois*–patterned stair runner speaks to the wood inlay floor. OVERLEAF: The collection of Han dynasty pottery (circa 200 BC to 200 AD) bridges the conversation between a circa-1770 giltwood mirror, a totemic 1969 Barbara Hepworth sculpture, and a 1959 painting by Richard Diebenkorn. A diagonally patterned floor is a classic device to direct the eye—and the body—into the adjoining rooms.

ABOVE: The entry hall's time travels continue with a late eighteenth-century Neapolitan marquetry commode surmounted by an ancient bronze vessel and a mid-twentieth-century artwork by Fujiko Shiraga. OPPOSITE: Conceived in concert with Skurman Architects, an enfilade of rooms with classical Louis XVI architectural elements, including reed-and-ribbon molding, spin history off from the entry. A reclaimed eighteenth-century *parquet de Versailles* floor provides an eloquent base for the living room's multicentury mix of furnishings and artwork. OVERLEAF: Under a Mark Brazier-Jones chandelier, the space divides graciously into three seating groups. Fabricated in England, custom-designed, intricately carved mantels of Ashburton marble anchor opposing walls. Flanking the chimney breast are George III mirrors, circa 1800, above eighteenth-century Italian marquetry commodes. Nearby, a sculpture by Antony Gormley speaks to paintings by Kazuo Shiraga (above the mantel) and Pat Steir (at right).

ABOVE, CLOCKWISE FROM TOP LEFT: Late seventeenth-century Chinese porcelain vases on eighteenth-century French bronze mounts sing in decorative harmony with a Hans Hofmann painting. Under one seating group, a Greek key-patterned rug resonates with the room's various elements of classical and neoclassical geometry. Its mate in the same subdued tones adds a contemporary flavor beneath an Italian parcel-gilt bench, circa 1800, and Ingrid Donat's handmade bronze coffee table. The antique commodes were found on a shopping trip to Rome. OPPOSITE: The powerful 1960 painting by Hans Hofmann provides a boldly arresting juxtaposition with a pair of Louis XVI fauteuils.

A painting by Albert Oehlen provides a striking focal point for the living room's third seating area, which centers on a contemporary bronze table by R&Y Augousti with shagreen and inset agate top. Flanking a tufted silk velvet banquette are an Irish George I gilt-gesso side table and one of a pair of hexagonal drum tables by Philip and Kelvin LaVerne.

PRECEDING: The dining room's Régence-period French boiserie paneling (bleached for a more California vibe), nineteenth-century Sultanabad carpet, original late eighteenth-century japanned "loop" chairs, and extraordinary Tuscan alabaster vases, circa 1840, resting in terracotta-colored niches, celebrate the fantastical theater of design history. **ABOVE LEFT:** The massive Qianlong cloisonné jardinieres, circa 1775, from Galerie Steinitz, provide a colorful counterpoint. **ABOVE RIGHT:** The flying camel and dragonfly-wing details of these Louis XVI sconces, circa 1780, charm on close view. **OPPOSITE:** The eighteenth-century Italian giltwood chandelier's scrolling form repeats a subtle decorative motif. Above a contemporary Ingrid Donat bronze console hangs a painting by Richard Diebenkorn from 1949.

**ABOVE:** In the library, the textures tell an organic story with bronze tabletops etched like tree rings, a wood grain–patterned velvet, and a Moroccan carpet with an irregular cellular geometry. **OPPOSITE:** The organic motif continues on the library's paneled walls, where a subtle *faux bois* paint treatment swathes the room in another rich layer. The marble floor's undulating fan pattern perfectly borders the rug's edge. The nineteenth-century giltwood-and-ebonized armchairs in the manner of Jean-Joseph Chapuis are a find from Carlton Hobbs. The silver tea-papered ceiling casts a magical glow. **OVERLEAF:** The curved banquette affords a glamorous window perch, with the 180-degree view stretching from the Golden Gate Bridge to Alcatraz Island.

28

ABOVE: A custom triple-tiered bronze pendant descends from a domed oculus cascading light into the house's core; like the stair rail that mimics the front door, it was fabricated in Paris by Ateliers Saint-Jacques. **OPPOSITE, CLOCKWISE FROM TOP LEFT:** The rare Portuguese eglomise mirror, circa 1880, inspired the design of this powder room with its hand-painted Gracie wallpaper, custom silver-backed glass moldings, shagreen-clad cabinetry, and trompe l'oeil inlaid-ivory woodwork. A 1957 painting by Joan Mitchell graces the entry to the powder room vestibule. An oval oculus adds architectural interest and a soft glow to the powder room. In the powder room vestibule, a wall sculpture by Ruth Asawa interjects a modern comment on the Tang dynasty horse and Han dynasty pottery.

OPPOSITE: With multiple exposures, the kitchen is filled with light throughout the day, a wonderfully functional and welcoming gathering space for the entire family. An adjacent scullery affords a separate area for preparation, storage, and post-meal cleanup. ABOVE: The kitchen opens to a comfortable, elegantly relaxed, and art-filled sitting room where family and friends can gather. The breakfast table sits in the window bay, an inviting spot for intimate or casual meals—and fabulous views.

On either side of the sitting room sofa, custom octagonal bronze tables with tops and shelves of Brescia marble offer a generous place to put down a drink or a book. The woodwork, glazed and dragged in shades of pale celadon, offers the perfect backdrop for Wayne Thiebaud's *River Lands*, 2004-2005. The custom leather ottoman anchors the seating group on an antique Oushak carpet.

ABOVE: In a hallway niche, Ingrid Donat's limited-edition bronze cabinet anchors a 1959 painting by Richard Diebenkorn. OPPOSITE: In a guest suite vestibule, a 1957 painting by David Park hangs above a George III serpentine-front commode, circa 1770, attributed to English furniture maker John Linnell. OVERLEAF: The primary bedroom's expansive view set the color palette, a mélange of soft blues, pale greens, and fog tones. Upholstered walls establish an air of serenity in this graciously scaled bedroom, which includes an intimate seating area. Above an eighteenth-century Italian lacquered cabinet hangs a 1958 painting by David Park. A petite Georges Rouault entitled *L'Asiate, dit aussi Orientale*, holds pride of place against the celadon walls.

ABOVE: From a floor of Avorio marble with an inset border of Breccia Oniciata to a glowing Venetian chandelier overhead, everything in the bath suite has an opalescent, luminous quality. **OPPOSITE, CLOCKWISE FROM TOP LEFT:** An eighteenth-century Italian commode found in Florence infuses the dressing room with an air of neoclassicism. Custom mother-of-pearl hardware created in collaboration with the Nanz Company heightens the glamour. In the marble-paneled shower, crystal knobs and a window just out of view amplify the radiance. Tang dynasty and Egyptian antiquities add to this room's feeling of timelessness.

The cool color palette of her study contrasts with the warm hues in Helen Frankenthaler's painting *Touch and Go*, 1977, which anchors one wall. An antique Tabriz rug grounds an Italian parchment desk by Aldo Tura, circa 1975. A truly extraordinary nineteenth-century French gilt-bronze and cloisonné pendant attributed to Ferdinand Barbedienne from Galerie Steinitz in Paris adds a unique enchantment. Behind the desk, shelves play host to personal artifacts such as a diminutive Georgia O'Keeffe from 1929, precious blue-and-white Chinese porcelains, and an antique Grecian torso.

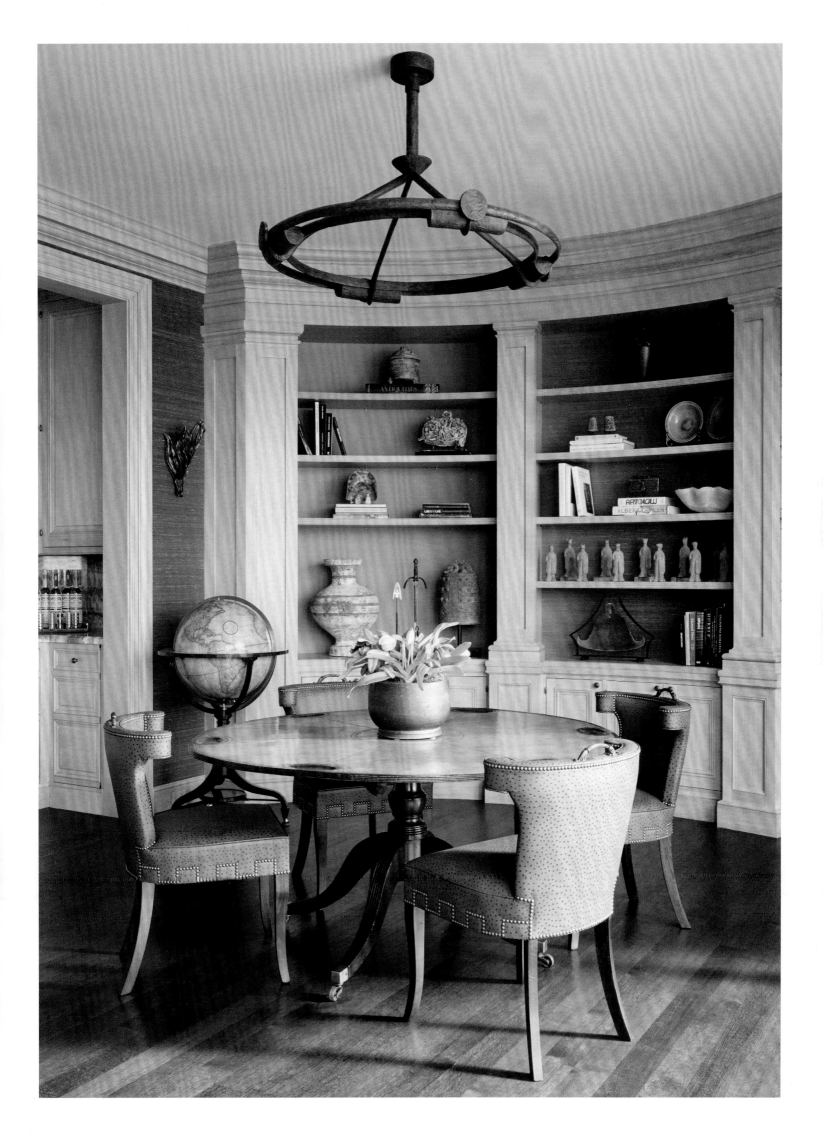

PAGE 46: A 1955 painting by Clyfford Still presides magnificently over the upper landing alongside a seventeenth-century Italian carved-alabaster vase (one of a pair). The tiered pendant light, which echoes the structure of the oculus and bronze stair rail, cascades like droplets into the stairwell. PAGE 47: Beneath a bronze lighting fixture by Philippe Anthonioz, a nineteenth-century English poker table surrounded by ostrich-covered casino chairs centers the action in an apse-like space that is part of the top-floor family/media room. Bleached white oak and raw silk walls envelop the room with a quiet textural presence. LEFT: Italian antique *lacca povera* slant-front desk and chairs set the tone in everyone's favorite guest room. The Persian Kermanshah carpet dates to around 1900. The color palette emerges from the two contemporary paintings, one by Per Kirkeby, over the desk, the other by Christopher Brown.

ABOVE, CLOCKWISE FROM TOP LEFT: The lower level includes a wine cellar, home theater, bar, and game room. At the wine cellar entrance, a mirror framed by marble specimens speaks to an embedded antique intarsia stone panel, a tabletop from a prior residence, and a 1949 console by Gilbert Poillerat. A gold-leafed ceiling and upholstered walls glamorize the home theater. The game room's custom-designed art deco-style straw marquetry walls, fabricated by Féau Boiseries of Paris, create a unique and inviting *club privé*. The adjacent bar continues the ebony and straw marquetry motif. OPPOSITE: A Louise Nevelson sculpture dominates a seating alcove; a cocktail table by Philip and Kelvin LaVerne and an antique Bakhtiari rug layer in more pattern.

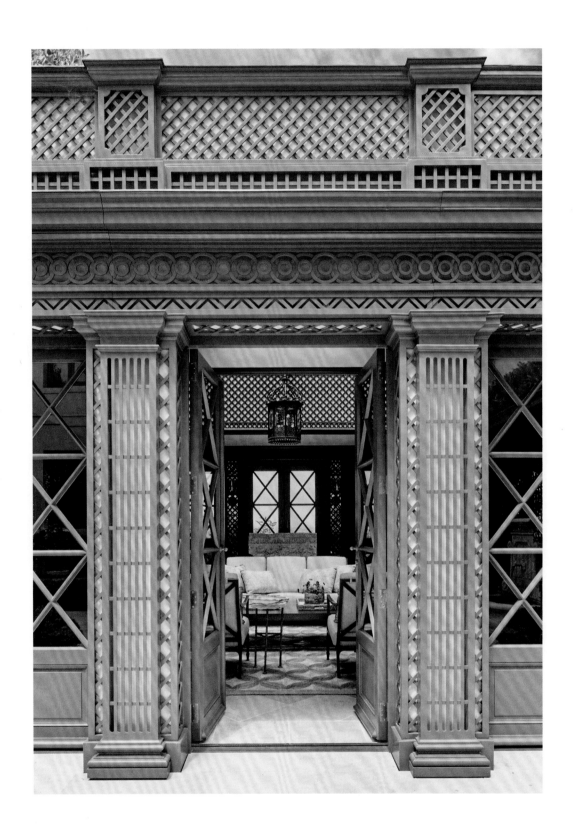

OPPOSITE: Converting a dilapidated carriage house at the back of the property into a Parisian-style pavilion added an extraordinary outdoor destination. A furniture plan with intentional flexibility results in a room that affords a variety of uses, from lounging to dining. Behind the custom treillage fabricated by Accents of France, mirrors magically create enchanting reflections. Hanging from a central skylight, the nineteenth-century English lantern, procured from the Rockefeller collection, features charmingly painted verre églomisé chinoiserie panels. ABOVE: The treillage-clad structure rises from the carriage house's original footprint.

# ROCKY MOUNTAIN HIGH

In Big Sky Country, nature's majesty presents itself at every turn. This house, seemingly carved into its remarkable landscape, called for interiors that felt equally compelling and organic. I am never one to shy away from the bold or massive, having learned from Michael Taylor not to allow it to intimidate a space—or me. Here, we looked for materials, textures, furnishings, art, and objects that met the scale of each space and the primeval drama outside. Yet these rooms still called for comfort and seduction. This we accomplished with the humanizing touch of the handcrafted and warm, earthy hues pulled from the surrounding terrain.

We established the interior's visual tone and conversation in the entry, with a harmonizing tension between rustic and refined. Here and throughout, hefty wood, iron, bronze, and leather play to and against massive stone walls. To anchor the living room, we designed a central table from a gigantic slab of petrified sequoia the client had found, and tempered the hard surfaces with luxurious upholstery, textural curtain panels, and overall tonal harmony. The dining room gave us the opportunity to insert a note of ethereal contrast with a spectacular pendant fixture of a forest of crystal trees that casts dappled light around the room and onto the table below. We complexified the textural epic further in the family room, adding layers of alluring tactility with woven rope furnishings, petrified wood tables, plush fabrics, an earthy leather rug, and several pieces of Aboriginal art introduced from the client's travels. The primary suite, children's bedrooms, and guest suites received the same welcoming palette of surfaces and colors.

Whether these clients visit during the summer months or at the winter solstice, their mountain house at eight thousand feet beckons with a modern, open lifestyle in a landscape from the beginning of time.

OPPOSITE: The interiors throughout feature refined earth elements in conversation with rugged sandstone walls. The entry establishes a grammar of scale, texture, and tone via a handcrafted walnut and iron console, a labradorite-studded 1980s French mirror, a custom-designed lantern, and bronze lamps with glass spheres. OVERLEAF: The procession of entry creates the illusion of indoor/outdoor living. A pair of Ethiopian shields and a leather-upholstered iron bench introduce additional organic elements into the materials repertoire. The painted and incised wood panel is by South African artist Lucky Sibiya.

PRECEDING: Sumptuously textured, luxurious fabrics with generously scaled patterns temper the hard surfaces of the great room, a vast space framed by a lofty pitched roof, expanses of glass, and enormous timbers atop stone pylons. A polychrome ceramic wall sculpture by Charles Sucsan, circa 1970, commands the fireplace wall. **ABOVE:** The coffee table incorporates a rare massive slab of petrified sequoia found by the client. Smoky quartz crystals inject timeless touches of glimmer. **OPPOSITE:** In the powder room, a wooden window grille serves as a counterpoint to the rugged texture of the "woven" travertine walls that flank the luminous, waterfall-like wood onyx vanity.

RIGHT: The durable and the delicate play off each another in the dining room. The one-of-a-kind Italian chandelier by glass artisan Simone Crestani mimics the living landscape. A French convex mirror with a welded brass frame adds yet another organic layer of rustic refinement into the mix. Handcrafted dining table, chairs, and walnut console ground the room in the resonant power of artisanship. OVERLEAF: A sectional sofa beckons in the family room, where the concert of textures harmonizes with a leather rug, a woven-rope lounge chair and ottoman, and *MMVI-II*, a fresco on linen by Marcia Myers.

**OPPOSITE:** Dining chairs with woven-leather backs pull up to a custom breakfast table with a totemic, inner-gilded bronze base. An Aboriginal artwork adds its mysterious song lines to the pattern story above a Tibetan painted elm cabinet from the 1920s.
**ABOVE:** A nineteenth-century Danish farm table—a natural resting place for a tableau of prehistoric ammonites, bronze ceremonial vessel lamps, and a wooden African headrest—fits perfectly along a living room side wall below a bronze mirror. A local craftsperson made the stool with antlers scavenged nearby.

**ABOVE:** The mood lightens in the vestibule outside the main bedroom. Integral-colored plaster walls, a perfect backdrop for artwork by Carol Pierce, take tonal cues from the house's sandstone walls. A graceful brutalist console hosts a leafy bronze table lamp. **OPPOSITE:** A tufted open-back banquette nestles into the window of the main bedroom, providing a magnificent perch without blocking the spectacular view. Columnar curtain panels are pocketed into the ceiling, emphasizing the room's height while also lending softness.
**OVERLEAF:** Striated onyx walls that suggest the layers of time and a limestone floor endow the main bath with an earthy, honey-toned lushness.

The study centers on a Swedish
modernist desk, circa 1934, by
Axel Einar Hjorth. A pair of 1960s
chairs by Edward Wormley plays
off the angular geometry of the
vintage French giltwood mirror and
the Aboriginal art over the
credenza; just below, a lamp made
of silkworm cocoons honors the
client's twelfth wedding anniversary.

OPPOSITE: Hand-hammered bronzed pendants with crystal balls march down the hallway that leads from the family room to the private quarters; Marcia Myers's *Color Journey MMVI-II* provides a striking focal point. **ABOVE:** A lighted "moon" art piece by Ben and Aja Blanc casts a luminous glow in the son's room. **OVERLEAF, CLOCKWISE FROM TOP LEFT:** An orbital pendant amplifies the celestial motif in the son's bedroom. Distinct personalities and color palettes differentiate the green and blue guest rooms. The daughter's bedroom incorporates her favorite wisteria and lilac tones, speaking to the local ceanothus "mountain lilac."

# A CLASSIC BEAUTY

**M**ost interiors resonate with memories and weave together those threads in a collaborative process. This Bay Area penthouse certainly does. These clients embarked on a full remodel down to the stud walls, introducing a Georgian vernacular into a classical Beaux Arts–style building with meticulously detailed spaces inspired by the work of Sir John Soane and Sir Edwin Lutyens.

Twelve-foot-tall ceilings beautifully enabled a new architectural layout that spun off all the spaces—the living room, kitchen, butler's kitchen, and bedroom suites—from a vaulted octagonal entry. The entry's inlaid marble floor was inspired by memories of my own travels, decades ago, to Kedleston Hall in Derbyshire, England, and, more recently, to Scotland's Manderston House.

With every inch rebuilt, from the walnut floors to the plastered ceilings, the concept was to color the elegance of the residence with the welcoming ease of an English country house. Flipping the existing living and dining rooms allowed us to add the family room and a mirrored dining alcove flexible enough for both formal and informal occasions. A serious cook, my client delighted in the newly positioned west-facing kitchen. And her request that we replicate the library from her grandparents' house inspired the family room, paneled in a rich Baltic pine stained and waxed to match the room of her cherished remembrance. Throughout, the clients' artwork, collections, and love of blue guided our choices.

Upholstered walls in her suite quiet city sounds and generate a soft glow throughout the day; the same pale, honeyed tones enliven the mosaic floor of her bath. In his mahogany-and-suede-clad suite, bold hues picked up from a rare antique carpet and the bath's graphic stone floor convey a decidedly masculine story.

With 360-degree views, this apartment effortlessly captures the beauty of light as it transitions from morning to night.

OPPOSITE: The entry hall sets the interior's overall tone. A beguiling design by Robert Adam for Kedleston Hall, and a similar one at Manderston House, inspired the floor pattern. Its five stones speak to the client's favorite hues, as do the celadon-glazed walls. The French Régence mirror, circa 1720, from a previous residence, adds sentiment and age into the mix, which includes a bronze console by British artisan Lucy Johnson. OVERLEAF: An early twentieth-century Tabriz rug and custom embroidered curtains suggest the living room's color palette. A massive Sean Scully painting presides over the custom Schiaparelli-inspired sofa. Stephen Antonson's plaster pendant plays off the surrounding geometries.

OPPOSITE, CLOCKWISE FROM UPPER LEFT: A charming Picasso plate rests atop R&Y Augousti's bronze nesting tables inlaid with shagreen and semiprecious stones. One of Hamish Mackie's sterling silver lobsters holds court atop a vintage Philip and Kelvin LaVerne coffee table that melds harmoniously with the Tabriz rug's tonal poetry. A peacock-blue crackle-lacquer side table provides a brilliant base for a tole flower sculpture by Vladimir Kanevsky. Dressed in crocodile cut velvet with a deep fringe, a versatile ottoman nestles under a late eighteenth-century marble-topped Italian console. ABOVE: Lee Ufan's acrylic-on-canvas work *Dialogue*, 2017, is juxtaposed with a seventeenth-century Italian Baroque commode.

OPPOSITE: The colors of the early nineteenth-century Tabriz rug harmonize with the azure tones throughout the room and the vista beyond. ABOVE: A quartet of eighteenth-century Piemontese neoclassical chairs surrounds the game table. Another of Vladimir Kanevsky's tole floral confections serves as a centerpiece. OVERLEAF: The hand-cast plaster ceiling unifies the living room's two seating arrangements. An English rococo mirror, circa 1755, commands the wall above the eighteenth-century Italian marble mantel, offering its reflections on time and place.

PRECEDING: For this client, a fabulous cook, the newly positioned west-facing kitchen takes pride of place. With dramatic quartzite counters and backsplash, hand-painted cabinets in a denim strié finish, and verdigris pendants, the room is a symphony of blues and grays. The Baltic pine island connects the kitchen to the adjacent family room. The French doors open to a wraparound balcony. **OPPOSITE:** The combination of decorative crosshatch and strié paint finishes by Stancil Studios enhances the paneling. **ABOVE:** The bar in the family room continues the conversation in Baltic pine and a fossilized stone countertop and backsplash.

ABOVE: The family room's pine paneling recreates a childhood memory of beloved grandparents' library. A rare nineteenth-century English convex mirror introduces an exotic note of Egyptomania. The custom marble mantel was made by Jamb in England. A drop-down screen converts the room to a home theater. OPPOSITE: Han dynasty vessels wired for lamps flank the sofa atop shagreen tables by R&Y Augousti. The artwork is by Tara Donovan, and the rug is an early twentieth-century Kerman.

ABOVE: A butler's pantry with commodious storage for china, linens, silver, and other essentials transforms the hallway to the second kitchen into a light, bright, and well-organized space. OPPOSITE: In the renovation, the apartment's standard east-facing kitchen became a much-needed second working chef's/catering kitchen. While more casual, it is highly functional, outfitted with professional-grade appliances to suit its use. Blue accent tiles instill the hardworking white space with crisp, fresh charm and visually tie it to the main kitchen.

ABOVE LEFT: In the entry foyer, silk velvet upholstery on a custom replica of a neoclassical bench slips in a warm tone to contrast with the cool pale blues and celadons. ABOVE RIGHT: The antique Italian textile on an early eighteenth-century Flemish walnut stool pulls up the rug's colors into the family room and reintroduces the living room's embroidery motif. OPPOSITE: An enfilade of arches, pendant fixtures, and patterned wood flooring coalesces in the main gallery. A custom, onyx-topped bronze console inserts a reference to nature in a niche opposite the powder room. At one end of the axis, Helen Frankenthaler's 1983 *Untitled* draws the eye.

The nineteenth-century Turkish Oushak rug gave rise to her bedroom's palette of warm and cool caramel tones, apricot hues, and honey colors. The tonalities gain resonance across a play of textures that combines velvets, leather, lacquered chinoiserie, custom embroideries on the curtains, bed hangings, and bed linens, and dainty passementerie. Upholstered walls set off by glazed, strié, and dragged moldings transform the space into a serenely luxurious, sound-dampening cocoon. The details of the custom chandelier inspired the ceiling's plaster tracery.

**ABOVE:** The cream chinoiserie lacquered vanity in her bath is just one of numerous pieces designed specifically for this project. Fortuny roman shades filter natural daylight so seductively. **OPPOSITE, CLOCKWISE FROM TOP LEFT:** Antiques like this eighteenth-century Danish rococo commode and George II mirror add a rich patina to her bedroom. The baldachino heightens the allure of her very romantic bed. A closer look at the seated vanity reveals charming hand-painted chinoiserie scenes. Her bath is an ultrafeminine retreat shaped by a barrel-vaulted ceiling and a mosaic floor infused with a paler, luminous version of the bedroom's honey and cream tones.

ABOVE: French-polished mahogany doors, moldings, and wainscot instill the secondary suite with a masculine spirit. RIGHT: With a color palette pulled from the nineteenth-century rug, the bedroom of the secondary suite explores the darker tones of blues, cocoas, and creams. The custom, crewel-embroidered curtain panels, a motif throughout, bring in the touch of the hand. Suede-upholstered walls tailored and defined by mahogany millwork create a glorious backdrop for a set of four early eighteenth-century hand-colored copperplate engravings of celestial charts from the book *Harmonia Macrocosmica* by Andreas Cellarius (Amsterdam, circa 1708). The lantern overhead picks up on the celestial theme.

ABOVE: A favorite shade of blue found in the Brazilian Azul Boquira quartzite takes center stage in the secondary bath. OPPOSITE: The intricate intarsia floor is a fantasia in contrasting stones that is loosely patterned after a surviving example from the Domus Aurea, the vast complex that Emperor Nero built on the Oppian Hill in the heart of ancient Rome. An eighteenth-century Italian Baroque walnut credenzina provides additional storage.

**ABOVE:** A "feathered folly," this jewel box of a powder room is enveloped with a feathered wallpaper. The undulating plumes inspired the choice of the bird-shaped fixtures, early nineteenth-century Viennese giltwood chandelier, and parcel-gilt, glazed ceramic mirror handcrafted by Eve Kaplan. The warmth of the gilt touches plays eloquently off the room's cool tones. **OPPOSITE:** The touches of blue and the conversation of textures that thread their way through the apartment continue in the guest bedroom.

# LIFE AT THE TOP

When these clients joined forces and left behind a traditionally decorated house and a classically appointed apartment for a contemporary, open-plan lifestyle, they took a leap of faith into a fantastic duplex penthouse. With expansive terraces and views from every room, it was perfect . . . except that it was a long, unfinished concrete shell with an industrial steel staircase smack in the middle of those remarkable views.

Vast, empty spaces speak to me of possibilities and opportunities. I always see the potential to create "bone structure," finesse the flow, and balance rooms. Working closely with the clients, we laid out the floor plan for maximum function and comfort, with sight lines and direct pathways from the kitchen, sitting area, dining area, and living room. Moving the staircase unblocked the view and made private the top floor of the master suite, his and hers studies, and a guest room. As we defined the wall planes and selected the finishes—unusual stones and reflective and matte surfaces—we highlighted their inspiring collection of artworks.

These clients embrace color, so in the kitchen we opted for drama, anchoring the space with a high-gloss, deep slate blue. For the bar, a jewel box tucked under the new staircase, we brought in a glow with seductively lacquered paprika-colored walls. To visually double the living room, we mirrored a full wall to reflect the opposing views and the onyx fireplace with its waterfall-like pattern.

Upstairs, favorite shades of green connect his study to the park it overlooks; for her, a ravishing redhead, glossy geranium makes her study the perfect cocoon. The serene master suite ties these threads together and spins them, with variations, into a master bath of dreamy bleached woods and subtle stones.

In this havenlike perch, warm and cool hues throughout contrast languidly yet subtly against the ever-changing sky and its beckoning vistas.

Keeping in mind that this project started as an unfinished concrete shell, the entry begins the transformation to an elegantly detailed present. A shallow barrel vault creates an illusion of height. Plastering the ceiling a subtle sky blue, an old Michael Taylor trick, enhances the sensation of loftiness and brings an outdoor reference to an enclosed interior. High-gloss paneled walls and a polished marble floor amplify the play of light. With vintage 1940s art deco Murano glass sconces, a contemporary brutalist mirrored console, faux shagreen mirror, and a 1930s French art deco bench, the entry sets the stage for the contemporary design drama to come.

When the opportunity presents itself to add a fireplace, as it did in this living room, it is only natural to make the most of it. Sheathing the entire chimney breast, mantel, and fireplace surround in cappuccino onyx creates a focal point that centers the seating group, incorporates the stunning view, and provides a magnificent backdrop for a commanding artwork by Zhang Huan and the flanking contemporary Italian wall sconces. The stone table is a vintage Michael Taylor piece that the client purchased in the 1970s when Michael designed his first house.

OPPOSITE: Mirroring the entire back wall of the living room is a favorite technique in narrow confines, creating the illusion of expansiveness and visually doubling the impact of the view. In this case, the mirror also provided an excellent place to float a large artwork by Agnes Martin. **ABOVE:** In the face of such vast vistas, the Moroccan rug serves to ground the living area. It is also an intrinsic part of creating the ambience of casual coziness. Vintage textiles introduce pattern and texture. A sculpture by Isamu Noguchi activates the corner.

**ABOVE:** The living, sitting, and dining areas flow naturally into one another in this apartment's expansive, open plan. Area rugs and furnishings anchor each separate space without compromising their relationship to one another or the view. The bronze horse sculpture by Deborah Butterfield takes in the scenery. **OPPOSITE:** Lifting the ceilings over the individual areas within the great room helped to create additional spatial differentiation, as did selective use of a high-gloss sheen overhead. Sheer wool panels at the windows filter the light without obscuring the views. The contemporary quartz crystal ceiling fixture offers an ethereal contrast to the more traditional furnishings below.

**ABOVE:** Beneath McArthur Binion's *DNA:Study*, 2019, a well-stocked Italian goatskin bar cart by Aldo Tura, circa 1960, indicates the entry to the bar, which is tucked under the stairs. **OPPOSITE:** Design solutions, such as this interior's mirrors and barrel vaults, can become elements that subtly tie together the entire spatial composition. With the bar, the challenges of the conditions dictated the bold response. The gold-leaf ceiling ups the glamour factor and the glow of reflected light; so does the saturated palette. The painting by John Currin is perfectly positioned to comment on the surroundings.

ABOVE: In a compelling conversation of patterns, colors, and textures, the space between the entry and new stair speaks to the nearby sitting area. The bark-papered walls, softening the contemporary lines of the apartment, afford a textural backdrop for a striking painting by Cecily Brown. OPPOSITE: A custom hand-painted wallcovering from de Gournay combines with a palette of murky deep greens, a glimmering glass mosaic floor, and a shimmery mirror wainscot to transform the powder room into an underwater fantasy. An art deco–style mirror reflects a ceiling light that floats like a lily pad overhead.

**ABOVE:** In the powder room vestibule, an artwork by Richard Diebenkorn draws the eye above the Georgian chest of drawers. Art deco touches in the stepped ceiling, custom grille, and snakeskin paper endow the rather traditional vignette with a certain soigné sensibility. **OPPOSITE:** Anchoring the east end of the floor plan is the open kitchen. Creating a highly reflective yet seductive tonality with glossy graphite cabinetry and moody cielo quartzite counters and backsplash, the kitchen takes on a glamorous vibe.

ABOVE: The fact that this residence is a penthouse meant the luxury of putting in skylights to open the primary bath to natural daylight. Bleached sycamore cabinetry, mirrors, and stone softly colored in flattering hues bathe the room in a gentle glow. OPPOSITE: Good fortune smiled again in the main bedroom, where it was possible to install a fireplace with a wood onyx mantel. Upholstered silk walls, a vintage 1940s Murano glass ceiling fixture, and 1970s Italian sconces combine with a contemporary Venetian mirror to create a room with spectacular views that is first and foremost a truly romantic retreat.

**ABOVE:** The windows in his study take in the expansive treetop views, which cued the use of green, a favorite color, on the millwork. Vintage textiles add texture and pattern to the custom daybed. The painting by Reginald Baxter seems to stalk a smaller version of itself atop the mid-twentieth-century desk by Michel Boyer. Mid-nineteenth-century Shanxi elm stools serve as coffee tables. **OPPOSITE:** In her study, the palette springs from the contemporary Turkish rug, with millwork finished in a rich, high-gloss coral and a red leather Marcel Breuer Wassily chair. An artwork by William Kentridge looms large beside a small portrait by Nathan Oliveira.

# ON CONTEXT

Every residence has an internal life and an external life. The process of design melds the two into a singular world. I always ask myself what suits a person and place, the nature of the location and its terrain and climate, how these particular people will live—not just the individuals who will inhabit the residence, but also their neighbors and the wider community.

Geography and location set obvious parameters. If the site or existing residence is in an enclave of Spanish-style architecture, a Japanese-influenced house would look entirely out of place. At the same time, I look to the terrain and the way the house sits on the land because these affect the outlook throughout the interior, which can dictate everything from the floor plan to the color palettes.

I find that a house's inward life has much to do with its circadian rhythms: with the flow of natural daylight throughout the rooms and its transitions from morning to night, there are countless considerations. Do we have the luxury of views or are they a challenge to manage? Do we account for light or lack thereof? Can I shift these rhythms with a color palette, create a desired mood, and marry all the various elements of design and decoration to shape the desired environment?

As I delve into my clients' way of living, I develop an understanding of how they want to feel in each space: their unique morning and evening rituals, their preferences for everything from meals to entertaining, from bathing to relaxing. Just as important are the personal inclinations in terms of the residence's public and private aspects. I am a big believer in creating maximum flexibility, so that the ability exists to open or close off areas as the situation warrants or as my clients want to expand and cocoon.

In America, because our built history is comparatively short, we tend to look overseas and to the past for architectural and design precedents: to England for a Georgian house, to France for Beaux Arts details, and so forth. Happily, we can study the originals, learn from the past, and determine what to carry forward. If the house is being built from scratch, a collaborative team is imperative to engage every detail to realize the client's dreams. When the givens are more fixed, such as with the remodel of an existing house or apartment, the history of the residence and other places like it can provide evidence and direction. When clients reveal no stylistic preference, then I delve even deeper into how they see themselves, how they want to be seen, how they want to live, and most important, what makes their heart sing.

The idea of soul, of appropriateness and context, is the lens through which I observe and filter my decision-making. Always, my goal is to make the visual captivate, seduce, and enchant.

# SURF'S UP

**B**each houses are always evocative of a carefree existence, filled with sun, sand, and sea, especially when paired with the best surf breaks along the California coast. When these clients told me they had purchased a "surf shack," my heart lifted. (I am a beach girl from way back.) The husband waxed rhapsodic about the location, the waves, the best time of year for the swells. That he mentioned little about the house itself spoke volumes. Indeed, it wasn't at all "them." The wife asked that the street-facing facade speak to the area's unassuming Spanish-style vernacular. They both wanted the Pacific-facing facade to have a contemporary look, glassed-in yet open to the spectacular views. An exterior face-lift and a complete interior gut and reconfiguration created an entrancing vista straight through the house, while arched doorways, hand-plastered walls, forged ironwork, and rough ceiling beams introduced an understated, modern Spanish flavor.

The family requested that the house enable a beachy bathing-suits-and-barefoot lifestyle. In the reproportioned great room and adjacent kitchen, we opened the entire rear wall to capture the endless horizon. Artisan pieces sourced from New York to New Orleans, Africa to Mexico, mix with California funky elements tossed into a cache of mid-1960s pieces. The surroundings inspired the sea-sand-sky palette of colors and materials suited to relaxed beachside living. Upstairs, in the bedrooms, we continued the casual melding of furnishings, textiles, and patterns to create unique yet cozy spaces. In the primary suite, we took full advantage of the ocean vibe and breathtaking views with earthy materials and a celestial blue stone in the bath.

The family's exceptional art holdings certainly raise this beach house's level of sophistication. Yet the house maintains its ease. Now it's with a knowing wink that we fondly refer to it as the "surf shack."

This interior's reinvention involved repositioning the stair to create a central path to the great room and frame an axial view from the front door straight through to the ocean. The entry hall also brings in touches of the Spanish vernacular that recast the exterior; among them are the arched front door, custom ironwork hand-forged by a local artisan, terracotta tiles, plaster corbels, and hand-troweled walls that provide a wonderful background for an extensive art collection including a large work by Paul Resika. An antique bone-inlaid wood bench introduces an understated flourish of exotic rusticity.

OPPOSITE: With repeated arches adjoining squared spaces, the interior spins a classic vernacular into contemporary mode. Vintage Moroccan rugs, wicker seating, and a ceiling pendant with cast bronze kelp leaves mix with antiques in an ambience of relaxed sophistication. **ABOVE:** In the kitchen vestibule, André Brasilier's 1972 *Promenade sur le rivage* speaks to the location. A seventeenth-century Italian refectory table provides a home for decorative rain forest baskets by Panama's Wounaan people. **OVERLEAF:** The great room tells the story of opening this entire side of the house to the surfside view. The organic textural elements in this room—from the handwoven rope armchairs with ikat cushions to the stone-topped iron coffee table, geometric wool rug, collected fossils and pottery—speak to a casual yet sophisticated beach lifestyle.

**ABOVE:** In the living room area, the color palette and textural language connect the interior to the landscape. Behind the linen-covered sofa, André Brasilier's 1999 *Exultate Jubilate* (*Le bain de minuit*) captures the spirit of place. The lamp bases are made from vintage wine presses.
**OPPOSITE:** In one corner of the living area, a cerused-oak and iron console provides additional display space for the client's diverse collections, which span the prehistoric to the present, including this painting by Raimonds Staprans. At the back of the sofa sits a nineteenth-century Italian Baroque table with intricate bone inlays.

**ABOVE:** A slate table from the 1970s has just the right heft, elemental geometry, and organic feel for the living room with its mix of rugged and refined textures. **OPPOSITE:** The opposite seating area for TV viewing centers on a coffee table by Paul Becker from the 1960s; its inset top of reconstituted stone is embedded with sea glass fragments. A French midcentury cerused oak console, early twentieth-century African Thebes stools, a Tarahumara polychrome vessel, and a pair of Ethiopian house posts show off the international power of artisanry and the handmade.

The Spanish vernacular reemerges in the kitchen with the use of colorful hand-painted tiles on the backsplash and wall and the plates on the hood. The light-filled, bright workspace with silver travertine counters and bleached white oak cabinetry is intentionally open to engage with the living and dining areas and the outdoors.

OPPOSITE: Upstairs, in the main bedroom's seating area, an artwork by Raimonds Staprans introduces a wash of color above a mid-twentieth-century French oak buffet topped by a pair of heavily textured bronze lamps with calfskin shades. Copper rain drum side tables cozy up to lounge chairs dressed in a sky-blue hemp fabric. **ABOVE:** The subdued hues of ocean, sand, and sky continue on the upstairs landing, where a skylight opens the barrel-vaulted ceiling to the heavens and the rhythmic arches energize the spatial flow. The artwork to the left is by James Weeks; at the end of the hall is a painting by Terry St. John.

OPPOSITE: The upstairs study overlooks a covered terrace. A colorful painting by Terry St. John commands the wall behind a linen-covered lounge chair. ABOVE: The vestibule leading to the dressing room and main bath takes an ethereal turn with light filtered through decorative fretwork. The custom carved doors that add texture throughout the house take their inspiration from a sixteenth-century Spanish original. A mid-twentieth-century Danish stoneware table lamp by Richard Kjaergaard adds an elegant earthiness atop the cerused oak table. A bloom of bird's nest coral mounted on a Lucite base brings in the wonders of the sea.

PRECEDING: The main bedroom takes full advantage of the open wall along the ocean side of the house, which is where the Spanish vernacular meets modern California. Maximum height was achieved with a pitched beamed ceiling, inviting airiness and light. A pair of French vintage commodes with translucent alabaster fronts flank the bed. A custom alabaster pendant carries the material overhead. OPPOSITE: Lined in slabs of honed Blue Ondulato marble, the shower à deux seems to merge cinematically with the sea through the picture window. ABOVE: Beneath a silver light fixture that resembles tangled kelp, the mosaic floor glistens. Bleached cabinetry, chiseled alabaster sconces, and antiqued mirrors contribute to the ethereal mood.

OPPOSITE, CLOCKWISE FROM TOP LEFT: In the blue guest bedroom, the driftwood hues and mix of refined and rustic textures continue to star. An Indian dhurrie rug covers the floor in a harmonious medley of color and pattern. A quill mirror layers in an element of the unexpected. A seagrass lounge chair reprises the interior's thread of textures taken straight from nature. ABOVE: A Moroccan brass pendant lends a touch of exoticism and an international flair to the blue guest bedroom, which takes the majority of its cues from the seaside surroundings.

**ABOVE:** This guest bedroom has a tribal theme, underscored by the carved headboard with embroidered upholstery and Kuba cloth pillow. A faceted mica ceiling pendant adds magical reflective notes from on high. **OPPOSITE:** The 1940s American tramp art mirror, vintage Kuba cloth covering the small stool, Swedish geometric wool rug, and ikat curtains are all in pattern conversation with the carved doors. A lyrical nineteenth-century Italian serpentine-front commode adds rustic patina and personality.

RIGHT: The guest suites share a common open-air terrace. Handmade hexagonal terracotta tiles create a sensuous surface underfoot. OVERLEAF: The back of the house goes full-on contemporary with wide expanses of glass on both levels that make the most of the view of sand and surf. The life of the house extends into the landscape with an outdoor room paved in limestone slabs and oriented around a firepit. The biblical olive tree, which was craned in, and which thrives in the sea air, brings in an example of nature's sculptural powers.

# NEW YORK STATE OF MIND

Interior design is an ever-evolving process. Whatever the context or style of a space, I am always looking at the layering of its elements, constantly editing and refining with a discerning eye so that each choice augments all the others, including, and sometimes especially, the art. This process becomes even more poignant when art takes on a featured role. The truth is that when handed world-class pieces, the designer should work to both compliment and complement. In other words, the design should recede to bring the main event, the art, forward. This urban sophisticate of an apartment, extraordinarily spacious by Manhattan standards, is just such a project.

In feverish New York, a haven of tranquility and personal expression can be a necessity. With this in mind, and working with the clients' exceptional art collection, we kept an open plan and used a cohesive palette of relative neutrals so as not to compete with the art or the spectacular views. The tonal consistency allowed for seamless transitions from the arresting gallery-like entry, down the generous hall, and into the voluminous great room, which spans the full width of the building. Within this vast room, we defined three discrete spaces: a living room/sitting area anchored by a massive Helen Frankenthaler painting, a dining area at the opposite end adjacent to the expansive kitchen, and a central sitting area offering invitation to both.

The neutral palette jumps into technicolor in the apartment's inner reaches. A brilliant peacock-blue credenza in the wife's office brings midcentury glamour and echoes those hues in the Moroccan rug and lamps. A massive work by Yayoi Kusama in the den shifts the kaleidoscope again, inspiring the room's touches of cinnamon velvets, nutmeg mohair, and blasts of brilliant orange. Balancing contrasts—what could be more New York?

In the entry gallery, Anish Kapoor's *Random Triangle Mirror* makes a dominant opening statement: an active visual and acoustical presence, it reflects its surroundings, appears different from every angle, and bounces sound waves off its faceted tympanic surface. Installed above a highly polished vintage French sideboard from the 1970s, it also offers a fascinating contemporary twist on the classic front entry vignette of mirror and console.

A swath of quiet limestone outlined with Belgian black marble accents replaced a distracting wildly veined marble floor, creating calm underfoot so that the art—including works by Milton Resnick (opposite the Kapoor) and Lee Ufan (on the center wall)—comes to the fore. The porcelain discs of Lindsey Adelman's light fixture echo the floor's luminosity. A quartet of sconces by Hervé Van der Straeten add to the reflective glow, and the iron stools by Philippe Anthonioz bring the space back down to earth. **OVERLEAF:** In the living room, ethereal whites—from Helen Frankenthaler's 1982 *White Spray* to Studio Drift's *Fragile Future* ceiling fixture with actual dandelions—coalesce into a richly textured environment that feels both of the city and a refuge from it. The ebonized floor provides a sleek grounding; bittersweet-chocolate velvet chairs and the custom shagreen-topped coffee table balance the pale elements. The twelve-foot ceiling allowed for the verticality of sheer wool curtain panels that are evocative of Romanesque columns.

OPPOSITE: With its celebration of the art of building, Piero Fornasetti's Architettura cabinet from the 1960s deserves its placement between windows overlooking some of Manhattan's most iconic and historic structures. **ABOVE, CLOCKWISE FROM TOP LEFT:** In one corner of the dining area, a painting by Toshio Yoshida hangs adjacent a sculptural torchère by Kelly Kiefer. A work by Oswaldo Vigas above a stool by Hervé Van der Straeten adds focus to a wall in the front sitting area. Nesting tables with petrified wood tops fold in an organic element. A Per Kirkeby painting brings its sunshine to the midsection of the living room's multiple seating areas, anchored by a Philip and Kelvin LaVerne coffee table.

RIGHT: In the dining area, leather barrel-back chairs offer relief from the corners and angles everywhere in view, including the Flatiron Building out the window, the Studio Drift dandelion pendant overhead, and the off-kilter grid of Victor Vasarely's *Bug III*, 1956-58, which commands one wall above a custom lacquered credenza that adds its own strict filigree into the graphic narrative. **OVERLEAF:** A quintet of faceted crystal pendants by David Wiseman introduce an element of functional jewelry as well as color into an existing kitchen that, by Manhattan standards, is as large as a football field.

ABOVE: The kitchen incorporates a small reading nook overlooking historic New York. OPPOSITE: An artwork by Ha Chong-Yuen activates a kitchen wall opposite the island, where counter stools dressed in bold printed calfskin elaborate on the surroundings. OVERLEAF: Upholstered walls cocooning the main bedroom in silk create textural play with a channel-quilted niche and kidskin headboard. Two visible panels of a triptych by Matthew Brandt bring a forest into view opposite the urban jungle. The silk velvet–covered bench by Franck Evennou, silk rug, and velvet-upholstered nineteenth-century armchair attributed to Maison Leleu elevate the textural conversation.

**ABOVE**: 1970s French table lamps by Maison Charles gleam atop a 1940s French parchment-and-oak cabinet. The art is by Chiyu Uemae. **OPPOSITE**: The seating area in the main bedroom tells a calming tale of pales with a custom lacquer coffee table, shagreen side tables, and a mesmerizing piece by Brazilian artist Adriana Varejão. **PAGE 174**: In her office, a Moroccan rug weaves in the dominant hue of the 1960s lacquered goatskin credenza. Atop it are a pair of 1970s French Lucite table lamps. The desk is a customized limited-edition design by Thomas Pheasant. **PAGE 175**: A duo of Murano glass lamps and a mixed-media work by Kwon Young-Woo carry the tone across the room.

ABOVE: A Murano glass ceiling fixture and a pair of sconces add personality and softness to the existing bath. OPPOSITE: The grass cloth-wrapped guest bedroom hosts another interesting assemblage that includes a 1970s Empire coconut-veneered side chair, a 1950s cabinet by Osvaldo Borsani topped by nineteenth-century stone vases from Thailand, and an artwork by Oswaldo Vigas. OVERLEAF: The painting by Yayoi Kusama signaled the pivotal direction toward dramatic colors and bold choices in the intimate media room, with a black cashmere sofa flanked by zebrawood side tables, silk velvet chairs, and an octagonal ottoman upholstered in tangerine cowhide. Grass cloth walls in a silvery gray, neither bright white nor too dark, balance all the saturated hues.

# THE UPSIDE OF DOWNSIZING

So many people cherish the elements of their home for the memories they hold. This client had lived for decades in a rather grand house with interiors designed in the eighties by Michael Taylor and later by me. She and her late husband had assembled some fabulous pieces of furniture along with a lovely art collection. We all treasured the magnificent pieces Michael had found or designed for her, not least an exquisite and rare pair of eighteenth-century Venetian mirrors and two five-foot-wide gateleg tables. When she decided to downsize, we had to determine which pieces to bring along, bid farewell to others, and design and source new pieces—all with the added layer of editing given that the scale of the new residence differed greatly from the old. Understandably, questions of practicality and sentiment came to the fore.

To create the desired flow and ease of entertaining, we opened the living room to capture views and casually embrace the family room, dining area, and kitchen. We introduced strong sight lines to reinforce the circulation. From the living room, these all land in the family room, where a dining table, brutalist pendant fixture, and circular mirror emphasize theater of the round. From the dining room, the sight lines reflect back to embrace the living room's flanking walls, which we reserved for the treasured Venetian mirrors.

Upstairs, we combined what had been his-and-hers dressing rooms and baths into one airy suite with a spacious, light-filled dressing room and a sparkling bath that captured the treetop views. As for the main bedroom, it was unusual to be downsizing yet find wall space generous enough for those broad gateleg tables. They remain as old friends, holding her treasured memories—with space for new ones, too.

Objects, and especially antiques, really do have meaning. When this client downsized from the home Michael Taylor had designed for her and her family decades ago, a rare, treasured pair of very large eighteenth-century etched Venetian mirrors headed up the wish list of pieces to bring along. That said, the scale of the new place presented a challenge. Fortunately, at one end of the living room, the perfectly balanced wall planes flanked a pair of French doors. Previously anchored by stone consoles and high ceilings, these mirrors are now given a more direct perspective as they perch above bronze benches.

**RIGHT:** The living room melds an early nineteenth-century Biedermeier table and seventeenth-century French limestone mantel with an exquisite Sultanabad rug circa 1860. *Untitled* (*Hill Street*) by Wayne Thiebaud makes for a compelling focal point. Custom embroidery climbs the leading edge of the silk curtains.

**OVERLEAF:** Opening one side of the living room to the family room resolved the spatial symmetry, improved the sight lines, created the perfect landing spot for artwork by John Register, and brought her love of color vividly into play.

ABOVE: The view back through the new opening on the left side of the dining room captures the entry of the house. OPPOSITE: A pair of museum-quality Chinese gilt-and-polychrome-lacquer chests, which date to the Ming dynasty (1368-1644), infuses the living room with history. Like some other pieces, the dining chairs also have a Michael Taylor connection, as they are reproductions of his original "matchstick" chair. One of the dining area's captivating circular elements is the torch-cut brutalist pendant light designed by Tom Greene, circa 1970.

OPPOSITE: The family room occupies the other side of the dining room/kitchen. The Bakhtiari carpet from South Persia, circa 1900, again proved the catalyst for the language of tone, texture, and pattern. ABOVE: With pine cabinetry, limestone counters, hand-scraped walnut floors, rope counter stools, and Holophane pendants, as well as a smattering of antique bowls and vessels, the kitchen provides warmth and coziness as well as function, transforming it into yet another inviting gathering place for multiple generations of visiting family and friends.

The main bedroom in her previous house was much larger, yet in a wonderful stroke of serendipity, this room had a wall wide enough to accommodate both her bed and her beloved bedside tables, a pair of massive, five-foot-wide gateleg beauties that Michael Taylor had modeled after an antique when he initially designed her former bedroom. This room also has the benefit of a windowed niche with a beautiful view that now houses a lovely bureau plat. The early twentieth-century Kerman area rug from Persia converses with the custom hand-painted Georgian-style Gracie wallpaper panels, created to look like an eighteenth-century scenic Chinese paper.

OPPOSITE: The renovation transformed a series of upstairs rooms into the graciously organized enfilade of spaces that combine to form her main suite of bedroom, dressing room, and bath. ABOVE: With windows on two sides, her bath luxuriates in natural daylight. Her vanity table takes ultimate advantage of its window position. Feminine touches of art deco style come through in the Lucite fan chair and shagreen mirror. The mosaic floor, with the subtlest of patterned borders, shimmers softly below.

**OPPOSITE:** This guest bedroom, one of two, leads out to a very pretty terrace. The Khotan rug laid down the essential parameters of the room's color and pattern choices, which the custom embroidery on the curtains and the vintage quilt further embellish. The headboard pulls the curtain pattern from the perimeter into the room's center; the checked pillows, bench seat, and bed skirt provide an eye-catching balance. **ABOVE:** The guest room includes a comfortable sitting area, just right for reading or casual conversation.

# LA DOLCE VITA

Design projects sometimes seem to follow the maxim that what goes around comes around. At other times, they feel like kismet. Occasionally, as in the renovation of this Italian Renaissance–style palazzo, the two are one and the same. Five years after I designed the living room for the 2007 San Francisco Decorator Showcase, the new owners commissioned a renowned team to reimagine the entire property. Italophiles to the core, these clients embraced the long process of endowing the house and garden with new life and twenty-first-century function while keeping the reinvention as classical as possible.

Throughout, we prioritized bringing in natural light while framing the views, creating an ease of flow with seductive sight lines, and shaping appropriate settings for the clients' magnificent paintings, sculptures, and antiquities. With the architectural team, we dove deep into the minutiae of historic Italian palazzos for inspiration—specifically Palazzo Chigi-Odescalchi, Palazzo Spada, and Palazzo Pisani Gritti—researching informative details from mosaics and intarsia floors to plaster ceilings and moldings.

On several trips to Italy, we sourced marbles, collected antiques, and engaged artisans to painstakingly craft bespoke textiles, furniture, lighting, and architectural elements, including a carved marble staircase. A palette of Giotto-like colors induced a Renaissance aura throughout. In the dining room, we grounded upholstered walls with a handcrafted marquetry wainscot beneath stenciled, distressed ceiling beams. Furthering the Italian flavor, a terrazzo floor with huge chunks of stone set the scale in the morning room. In the kitchen/breakfast room, we subtly stenciled the ceiling coffers to hint at life under a Tuscan sun. For consistency, the primary suite's serene palette extended into the Italian stonework, intarsia floors, and mosaics by a local artisan. Excavating under the house, we added bedrooms, a wine cellar, a gallery, and the pezzo forte, a natatorium complete with dripping grotto. *Viva l'Italia!*

OPPOSITE: The client's preference for curvilinear and floral Italian motifs sparked the concept for this custom bronze door, fabricated by metal artist Michael Bondi. The pattern was inspired by a historic precedent. Flanking the front door is one of a pair of late nineteenth-century wrought-iron consoles from the de Guigné collection. OVERLEAF: Italian marble artistry features in the entry stair and the inlaid floor loosely based on one at the Vatican's Sala Regia. Stuc Pierre plaster walls set off an eighteenth-century Venetian mirror and late eighteenth-century Roman console. A custom tole lantern drops through the stairwell. An Alberto Giacometti bronze, *Grande femme assise* (*Annette assise*), looks on from the corner.

OPPOSITE: A room large enough for a pair of chandeliers, in this case a duo of eighteenth-century Italian giltwood and glass bead beauties, is a gift to a designer, especially when the project includes a renovation down to the studs. This living room takes its rich palette from the early twentieth-century northern Persian Tabriz rug. Walls upholstered in custom linen damask envelop the space. **ABOVE:** Flanked by an unusual pair of nineteenth-century Chinese export porcelain urns, Pablo Picasso's *La Lettre* (*La Réponse*) draws the eye above an eighteenth-century Italian inlaid commode. The nineteenth-century Louis XIV–style fauteuils are upholstered in a verdure tapestry.

OPPOSITE: In one corner of the morning room, next to a custom L-shaped banquette placed to bask in the sun, a rare eighteenth-century Italian center table shows off its exquisite marquetry. Custom embroidered curtains pull up the colors from the early twentieth-century Persian Tabriz rug. **ABOVE:** An unusually large-scale mid-nineteenth-century French bolection marble mantel creates an ideal hearth for gathering round, aided by a pair of custom swivel chairs and vintage hexagonal side tables by Philip and Kelvin LaVerne. A mid-eighteenth-century Italian gilt mirror suits the proportions of the fireplace wall. Camille Pissarro's *Les Peupliers, Matin* enchants above an eighteenth-century Venetian demilune console.

OPPOSITE: In the morning room, a custom hand-carved Istrian marble mantel reimagines a nineteenth-century English Italianate original; the two deep side panels carved with a pomegranate motif resolve a challenging spatial condition. The peripheral ceiling pattern, which frames the nineteenth-century *ombre latte* Murano glass chandelier, was executed by decorative painter Philippe Grandvoinet and his team and takes cues from several precedents: a drawing by Jules-Edmond-Charles Lachaise in the Metropolitan Museum of Art, combined with a series of details from the guest house at the Villa Valmarana ai Nani in Vicenza. Underfoot is an early twentieth-century Tabriz rug atop a custom hand-selected large-scale terrazzo floor. **ABOVE:** Alberto Giacometti's bronze *Bust of Annette* charms on an Italian inlaid marquetry gateleg table.

**ABOVE:** Transforming a niche into an event, Pablo Picasso's *Tête de femme (Portrait de Françoise)* commands the wall above a custom stone-topped console. **OPPOSITE, CLOCKWISE FROM TOP LEFT:** *Grande femme assise (Annette assise)*, a bronze by Alberto Giacometti, observes quietly from a corner. A nineteenth-century Venetian giltwood and etched glass mirror rises above an Italian marble-topped console table, circa 1785. An Apulian red-figure volute krater attributed to the Baltimore Painter, circa 330–320 BC, fills an intimate niche. *Man Under Tree*, a drawing by Camille Pissarro, anchors the wall above a Louis XVI walnut-and-tulipwood chest, in the manner of Maggiolini. The small bronze sculpture, *Despair*, is by an unknown artist.

PRECEDING: The dining room takes inspiration from an ideal of the Italian palazzo with marquetry wainscoting, walls upholstered in rich cinnamon silk, Fortuny curtain panels, marble floors, and stenciled ceiling beams. Eighteenth-century Italian twin chandeliers cast sparkling light that visually expands the room's confines. Nineteenth-century Italian giltwood pricket sticks flank Peter Paul Rubens's *Portrait of a Lady* above the sideboard. **OPPOSITE:** A Murano glass chandelier hangs over the breakfast table. Nineteenth-century Italian sconces illuminate the wall beside David Park's *Half Nude in Water* (*Water & Canoe*). **ABOVE:** Deep coffers and stenciled details activate the kitchen ceiling. The custom-painted tile and hand-hammered copper hood are reminders of bucolic Italy.

**ABOVE:** A custom-designed, antiqued tole tapered lantern descends in two tiers from the domed cove at the top of the stairs, an architectural centerpiece created during the renovation that allows light to wash through the core of the house. **OPPOSITE:** Under a barrel vault with a laylight, a series of alabaster pendants light the hallway to her study and a guest bedroom with a suffused glow. An alabaster sculpture of entwined figures occupies a gallery niche. At the end of the hall, René Magritte's *La magie noire* hangs over a nineteenth-century Portuguese rosewood *mesa bufete*.

PRECEDING: The opportunity existed to raise the bedroom ceiling to fifteen feet. The carved walnut bed meets the scale and is dressed with a nineteenth-century Portuguese Castelo Branco embroidered coverlet. Théo van Rysselberghe's *Esquisse pour l'heure embrasée* adorns the wall above the hand-carved Breccia Oniciata mantel between late nineteenth-century Venetian rock crystal sconces. Camille Pissarro's *Vue sur le village* hangs above an Italian commodino, circa 1750, between the windows. Milton Avery's *Pensive Sitter* occupies an intimate corner. OPPOSITE: The marble and intarsia floors were handcrafted in Italy. A domed ceiling creates a serene spa-like atmosphere with the champagne-colored Venetian chandelier. ABOVE LEFT: Luminous surfaces combine in her lacquered vanity table, shagreen mirror with silver-gilded border, and rock crystal table lamp. ABOVE RIGHT: The onyx-lined shower overlooks the bay with a window preserved in the renovation.

ABOVE: The library sitting room features a barrel-vaulted, plaster-coffered ceiling with opposing oculi that direct reflected light into the room via a system of mirrors. Aristide Maillol's bronze *Petite Flore nue* stands on the hand-carved Breccia Pernice mantel beside Paul Signac's *Antibes. Soir.* RIGHT: A Venini chandelier from the 1930s hangs over a seating group that arrays a sofa, hand-carved fruitwood chair, deep lounge chair, and oversize ottoman around a glass-topped coffee table. The rug is a Persian Tabriz, circa 1900. The millwork incorporates the molding motif seen throughout much of the house.

**ABOVE:** The client commissioned the watercolor by Gary Bukovnik that anchors the wall over the late nineteenth-century Louis XVI-style mantel in this guest bedroom. **OPPOSITE:** With upholstered walls and custom embroidered curtain panels in shades of peach, pale pink, and cream, this guest bedroom is a lush, inviting, soothing cocoon. The molding is glazed in the same tones, which adds to the effect. Gold accents in the bed's japanned finish and the late eighteenth-century giltwood chandelier gleam. A contemporary Oushak-style rug adds softness underfoot.

ABOVE: The custom-designed door to the wine cellar on the lower level was produced by Michael Bondi; like the front door, it shows the mastery of a true artisan working in bronze. OPPOSITE: Descending from the main entry hall, the lower gallery features Stuc Pierre walls, intarsia marble floors, and the entrance to the wine cellar.

RIGHT: It was necessary to excavate down two stories to create the space for the natatorium and grotto. The travertine floors throughout incorporate custom mosaics inspired by Roman archaeological sites and Byzantine tilework, and were painstakingly fabricated by artisan Pippa Murray. The Navona stone central grotto was hand carved in Italy with fantastical dolphins. PAGE 226: A custom lantern hangs above the spa. The decorative painting by Stancil Studios on the frieze was based on a sixth-century BC Lydian tile fragment seen in the Metropolitan Museum of Art. Holding court over the spa is a shell-encrusted bust made in the 1950s by French artist Janine Janet for the atelier of Cristóbal Balenciaga. PAGE 227: On the opposite side, a sumptuous seating area beckons.

# ON CULTURE

Design may be a language without words, but it speaks directly to our deepest human experiences—of our individuality, our personality, and our family. Offering an infinite spectrum of approaches, design can convey an endless wealth of information about who we are, what we dream of, and what makes us happy, comfortable, and at home.

I see the elements of design as a constantly evolving continuum, a broad, multifaceted take on the kaleidoscopic concepts of heritage, history, and culture. This lens offers me insights into a particularly layered idea of identity: one remembered or imagined, perhaps even aspirational. It also provides me with a creative framework for translating meaningful details of background and daily rituals into a living environment without seeming or being obvious or trite. I might occasionally give a wink here or a nod there to the specific background of the clients, but, more likely, I will develop a conceptual interpretation of their cultural heritage that will, on a subliminal level, make them feel at home.

Unearthing what a particular person or family is after involves asking countless practical and esoteric questions to peel back the layers in order to reveal how they live, what matters to them, and what resonates with them; perhaps even to uncover aspects of themselves that they may not know. This excavation process—part archaeology, part anthropology, part psychology—is what I see as the essential work of the designer.

So many people find comfort in the familiar, especially as they move someplace new.

Some people have personal touchstones they carry forward—remembered rooms, favorite pieces of family furniture, objects and art, particular colors—while others do not. Either way, exploring the memories of childhood can lead to revelations about dreams and the emotions that sparked them: the bunk beds they did not grow up with, but want for their children; their grandparents' pine library that provided a comforting haven; a stylized love knot that might serve as an ode to their romance. Such recollections also speak to heritage and identity. There are ever so many ways to embrace them, to transport them from one aspect and stage of life to another, whether through that piece that must come along because it is a treasured travel memento, a family touchstone, a sentimental inheritance, or the first painting a couple bought together decades earlier.

Design, in my view, is a means of storytelling, a way to capture and express identity, individuality, personality, and personal history in evocative yet completely tangible terms. My innate curiosity sends me constantly searching for answers to the storyteller's five basic questions: who, what, where, when, and why. Identity is truly one of life's conundrums. The more we study and try to parse that individuality, the more nuanced, complex, and layered our understanding of it becomes. Design allows me to translate visually these facets of identity and personal culture, to create all the particular comforts of home within a specific environment that ultimately reflects each person and family in all of their complexities.

# PANAVISION

The elements of design offer so many ways to enchant. Light, both natural and artificial, is among the most compelling, challenging, and rewarding. In this contemporary Southern California house, the daily dance of the sun's rays and contrasting shadows truly work their magic. The minimalist architecture prioritizes an enfilade of spacious volumes, commanding vistas from space to space, contrasting textures, magnificent views out to the landscape, and indoor/outdoor living.

With large rooms, I always ensure that they are as comfortable and inviting for two as for twenty. I stand by the principle that the ideal living room has three seating groups. Even when this is not attainable, my goal is to create intimate environments for conversation within large volumes enhanced by sumptuous materials and seductive lighting. In this living room, we created two distinct spaces for gathering, one more focused on the views, the other more centrally attuned to the fireplace. These cozier seating areas, each defined by luxurious rugs and generously scaled furnishings, beckon with a welcoming contrast amid the hard architectural surfaces. Throughout, we revamped the lighting to alter the evening mood.

Having learned from Michael Taylor, the maestro of scale, I strategically brought the outdoors in with several massive trees and exotic plants. Adding a few antique rugs and vintage pieces also instilled a wonderful tension through the juxtaposition of new and old. These also spoke beautifully to the client's centuries-spanning collections, from massive ancient fossils and antiquities to fantastic contemporary art.

Upstairs, the primary suite basks in magnificent views with fully opening window walls only achievable in warm climates. Lush textures, gauzy sheers, and a softened color palette helped transform these spaces into an ethereal sanctuary of plushness and comfort—a private retreat that makes the most of Southern California's remarkable, luminous light.

OPPOSITE: Spectacular views and the Southern California ease of living are the driving features behind the design of this residence, which facilitates seamless transitions between the interior and exterior spaces. OVERLEAF: The textural play of carved console, vintage rock crystal lamps, Murano glass mirror, perforated bronze ceiling fixture, tufted custom bench, and chiseled stone planter forms a serene counterbalance to Hung Liu's powerful *Manchu Bride–Buddha's Hand.* The sculptural black olive tree brings an element of the exterior inside. An antique Sultanabad rug lays a groundwork of pattern on the limestone floor that flows throughout the house.

PRECEDING: In the first of the living room's two seating groups, deep lounge pieces combine with a hand-knotted area rug in silk and wool and towering fishtail palms to create an inviting, cozy space for curling up in comfort. Barlas Baylar's chandelier of handblown Murano glass bubbles pulls the eye upward. **ABOVE:** A magnificent prehistoric ammonite offers a textural counterpoint to the contemporary architecture and speaks to the client's passion for history and archaeology. **OPPOSITE:** A custom onyx-topped coffee table centers the seating. Along the wall, a shagreen-topped demilune by R&Y Augousti works like a piece of jewelry. Petra Cortright's *Qam qbasic demodulator routledger69* surmounts the fireplace.

PRECEDING: The living room's second seating area, oriented to the exterior, incorporates barrel-back chairs with the sofas in response to the architecture's strict geometry. The textile mix blends seductively tactile bouclés and woven silks. A custom silk area rug adds softness and shimmer underfoot. An elongated version of the Barlas Baylar chandelier directs the eye into the landscape. Contemporary ceramic table lamps speak to the color of the sky. **OPPOSITE, CLOCKWISE FROM TOP LEFT:** A Miocene-age fossil of sea urchins is a powerful focal point. One of two Valiant chandeliers with handblown Murano glass bubbles by Barlas Baylar draws the eye to the view beyond. A red-figure knob-handled patera, fourth century BC, invites a closer look. A signed 1960s pewter, bronze, and enamel table by Philip and Kelvin LaVerne evokes a conversation in celadon. **ABOVE:** A Roman marble bust of the Empress Crispina as Omphale, Queen of Lydia and second wife of Heracles, dates to the late second century AD.

In the epitome of the indoor/outdoor lifestyle, the dining room features two pocket walls that open the space to the vista. A pair of Italian handblown demisphere pendants by Simone Crestani, curvilinear dining table by Hélène Aumont, and barrel-back dining chairs soften the architecture's geometry.

OPPOSITE: The breakfast area's custom walnut table with bronze "wishbone" legs sits underneath Carlo Nason's Artichoke lamps from the 1970s. The painting—*Portrait d'une élégante portant une robe de cour chinoise*, circa 1925, from the French school—lends a colorful touch. ABOVE: The family room's sumptuous seating ranges around a creamy lacquer coffee table. The crystal teardrop ceiling fixture adds sparkle above the custom silk and wool rug. OVERLEAF: His office expands into the garden, a connection reinforced by the botanical motifs of the Tabriz rug, circa 1920. The glass-topped desk with hand-sculpted bronze legs by Hélène Aumont is juxtaposed with a pair of custom barrel-back anigre and maple chairs.

OPPOSITE: In the main bedroom, a nineteenth-century French Venetian-style mirror hangs above the serpentine-figured ash credenza. ABOVE: Circular motifs add a distinct softness to the bedroom's vestibule, with a mirror surrounded by Venetian glass leaves above a curvilinear console with striated blush onyx top and silver leaf orb. OVERLEAF: Glamorous and alluring, the main bedroom emphasizes soft lines, soft tones, and the soft touch. Sheer wool casements filter the light. The custom hand-tufted silk area rug lays a plush foundation for the bed and swivel lounge chairs. The vintage plaster ceiling fixture harks back to the Hollywood Regency style. A Roman marble bust of a goddess, first-second century AD, gazes from atop the credenza.

OPPOSITE: The vestibule to the bath plays the dark off the lightness ahead, modulating the spatial experience. A 1970s Murano glass mirror hangs above the console of wood onyx and sculptural bronze. ABOVE: Sleek and minimal, the bath celebrates the compelling views, to which it also opens. The walnut saber-legged bench with scrolled details is upholstered in leather.

# A VIEW TO A THRILL

Every project calls for its own style of fusion. For this Bay Area pied-à-terre with an almost panoramic view, the client initially intended to retain the existing interior, a 1970s renovation with elements of the original 1950s architecture—an idea that rapidly gave way to the desire for a timeless space that maximized the spectacular vistas. We melded the couple's international backgrounds into the remodel, infusing the spaces with luxe materials from six different continents.

To complement the vistas, we reorganized the rooms with subtle but exotic materials—onyx, zebrawood, wenge, Kuba cloth, white jade, lacquer, silk, rich leather, and more—that blend in a multicultural harmony. We began introducing the couple's story in the sycamore-paneled elevator vestibule with a vibrant red "good luck" cabinet and, at their request, created an infinity-patterned marble floor for the entry, a contemporary take on the ancient Chinese love knot. We extended the rich materials into the living room and visually doubled the space with a mirrored wall. The dining room's bark-papered walls set off a commanding painting by Nathan Oliveira, purchased for the apartment, which inspired the chairs' spice-colored leather. In the library/family room, a nineteenth-century Japanese screen magically splits, rolling aside to reveal a large television. In reconfiguring the galley kitchen for easy daily function, we took a neutral approach to heighten the morning light. A procession of pilasters down the lacquered gallery defined landings for a coat closet, a powder room with African furnishings and materials, additional hidden storage, and, finally, the residence's private realm. In the primary suite, the discovery of a previously hidden window allowed us to create an ethereal bed wall with a patterned grille and gossamer curtain.

Design's expressive powers revealed this couple's worldly experiences through the fusion of diverse materials and tranquil colors, enhancing the excitement of living sky-high.

The elevator vestibule introduces motifs that recur throughout this residence. The circular door panel corresponds to the inlay in the multistone floor pattern of the foyer. Bleached, book-matched sycamore paneling conceals additional storage. The "good luck" red lacquer chest is a welcome greeting.

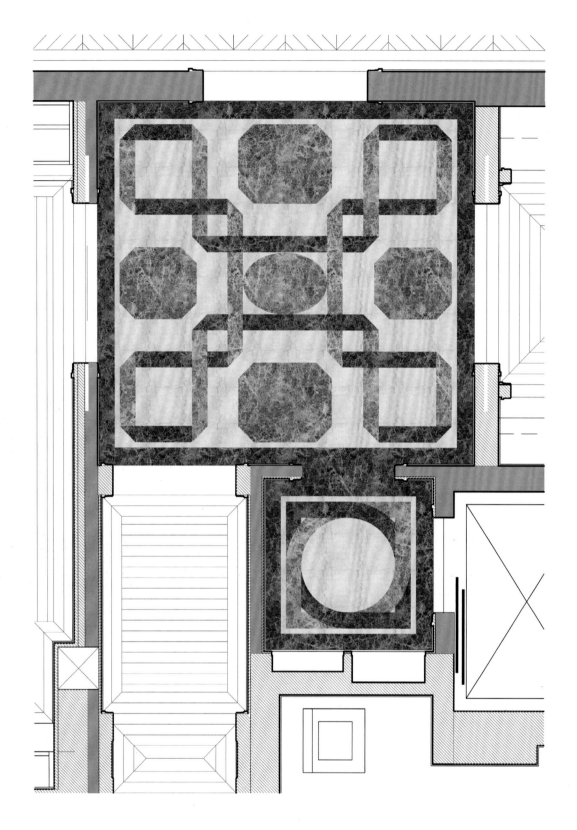

ABOVE: At the client's specific request, the unique and intricate inlaid floor designed for the entry interprets the Chinese love knot, the symbol of eternity, through a contemporary lens. OPPOSITE: In addition to the unbroken floor pattern in onyx and marble, the foyer expands on the circular theme with the bronze wreath pendant fixture and introduces one to the various living sections of the house. OVERLEAF: In the living room, the architectural conditions prevented physically raising the ceiling height. Many elements—including the fireplace wall done entirely in a waterfall-like striated onyx and the absence of moldings at the crown—emphasize the vertical while simultaneously playing up the cinematic view.

PRECEDING: Raising and widening the passage between the living and dining rooms created a more gracious flow and simultaneously directed the eye to the dining room's commanding painting by Nathan Oliveira. Custom parchment cabinets, one doubling as a bar, flank the entry. Bark paper–covered walls in the dining room introduce an organic texture. **OPPOSITE:** A circular table in the living room serves for intimate dining or games. **ABOVE:** The powder room expands on the multicultural mix with a mélange of exotic woods, including wenge and zebrawood, and a stylized floor border inspired by Kuba cloth. The art is Henri Matisse's *The Sword Swallower*.

263

PRECEDING: Paneled in bleached walnut, the library/media room incorporates inviting seating and an antique Japanese screen that splits and glides behind the bookcases to reveal the TV. **ABOVE:** A Murano glass and brass chandelier crowns the bespoke dining table with a flourish. An African mask and an onyx specimen bowl are part of the eclectic mix. **OPPOSITE:** The east-facing galley kitchen, which opens to the dining room and to the foyer, is bathed in morning light. Bleached wood and metal create a harmonious contrast of cool and warm tones.

PRECEDING: The main bedroom is a study in romantic serenity with a tone-on-tone palette. A previously hidden window behind the bed was uncovered during the renovation; the fretwork grille filters light and, combined with the fabric insert in the kidskin-upholstered bed, creates a semblance of privacy. An aquatint by Richard Diebenkorn graces the wall. **ABOVE**: Between bedroom and bath, a private dressing room allowed space for a built-in desk. **OPPOSITE, CLOCKWISE FROM TOP LEFT**: Patterns converge in the main bedroom. Quiet tones and understated hues dress the guest room. The main bath's bleached maple cabinetry complements the ivory onyx counters. The undulating book-matched honey onyx in the shower enhances the stone's organic striations.

# A CASE FOR KISMET

As a child growing up in a close-knit community of the then-small town of Santa Barbara, I roamed freely through neighbors' gardens and properties. There were no closed gates in Montecito back then. A tall hedge or a wall was an invitation to explore what lay beyond. Had I not been my curious self when looking for a rental property thirty years ago, I would not have sought out what was behind a hedge with a wooden gate that caught my eye from the car. The property spoke to me the moment I entered. I had discovered my enchanted garden, with wonderful old oaks, towering cedars and redwoods, magnolias, and giant bird-of-paradise palms, all filtering a dappled light. Without even seeing the house—as it turned out, a tiny two-bedroom, two-bath retreat with a lovely lap pool—I said I would take it.

In the years since we purchased our serene, happy place, we have created further secret gardens for dining and meandering. The structure of the house, however, we have left unchanged. The pool side opens onto a tranquil lawn, outdoor dining, and a beautiful mountain view. On the back side, where the terrain slopes down, balconies look up into the trees. The house started life as a bungalow, probably built in 1909 for the field hands who tended to the original forty-acre citrus grove. The late designer James Northcutt gave the house its first charming face-lift. We have decorated it for ease—a blend of simple surfaces, canvas slipcovers, accents of blue and white, and a few sentimental pieces, including an antique mirror from Michael Taylor's house—as a peaceful sanctuary from what I do every day for others.

Discovering this property on a random drive-by still feels like kismet to me. From the very first time I stepped into the garden long ago, I knew I was home.

Behind tall hedges and wooden gates, the entry to the property is a slow reveal. A meandering pathway through the front garden leads to a secondary doorway that opens to the loggia, the house, and the secret gardens beyond. The olive trees, rosemary, gardenia, strawberry guavas, *Osmanthus, Pittosporum crassifolium,* and *Podocarpus* trees are an orchestrated symphony of various greens. The pots insert accents of terracotta. The dappled light changes the mood from dawn to dusk.

ABOVE: A small alcove off the living room doubles as a writing nook, overlooking the sculptural oaks in the garden beyond. OPPOSITE: This is somewhat sophisticated bungalow living, so a casual blue-and-white palette feels fresh, appropriate, and restful. In the whitewashed living room, an exposed structural ceiling creates an airy loftiness. Antiques meld with slipcovered contemporary pieces, with nothing too precious. Above the eighteenth-century French limestone mantel hangs a Louis XVI mirror, a sentimental piece that belonged to Michael Taylor.

**OPPOSITE:** The charmingly compact kitchen is functional and airy. Bleached and glazed white oak cabinetry gives the space a warm, luminous quality, especially with wraparound windows that frame a perfect spot for the bar cart. A fun collection of baskets nests in the eaves, adding texture overhead. **ABOVE:** The outdoor dining terrace under the loggia is embraced by its living architecture. The convex mirror reflects light beautifully. A Corinthian capital serves as the table base.

The main bedroom opens to a south-facing porch that nests in the garden's upper story. The four-poster bed responds to the ceiling height; the embroidered bed hangings emphasize the verticality. The antique Swedish chest adds patina into the room's play of blue and white. The charming hand-colored engravings of birds by Albin with whimsical painted frames date to 1736—and are just right for this room in the treetops.

**ABOVE:** The garden contains several seating areas, all furnished for comfort from day to night. **OPPOSITE:** The guest bedroom, just large enough for a pair of twin beds, opens off the living room and looks out onto the tranquil porch. Patterns varying in scale and detail are happily unified by the consistent shades of blue and white. Vintage iron beds incorporate hangings, creating a cozy cocoon. A vintage Indian dhurrie rug covers the floor.

The pool, a destination in and of itself, also serves as a connector to other tranquil areas in the garden. Its width mirrors the width of the house. Potted kumquat trees add flashes of color when fruiting. The sculptural magnolia tree that centers the length of the pool speaks to the poetry of nature.